PEGASUS

AS TOLD BY
MARIANNA MAYER

ILLUSTRATED BY
K. Y. CRAFT

MORROW JUNIOR BOOKS
NEW YORK

Acknowledgments

While researching the Pegasus myth, two authors' works
proved to be most important: *The Greek Myths: Books 1 and 2* and *The
White Goddess*, written by the intriguing and insightful Robert Graves,
and the works of the scholar Erich Neumann—particularly *The Origins
and History of Consciousness*, a masterful work that uses the Greek classics
to seek a better understanding of mythology through the evolution of human
consciousness.

Many thanks to my research assistant, Karen Arm at the
Archive for Research in Archival Symbolism in New York City, for her
enormous help in gathering evidence from the Jung Center's Kristine
Mann Library to support my theories regarding the fraternal relationship
between Pegasus and Bellerophon. Although the hero and the horse had
different mothers, they were both sired by the same father—the sea god
Poseidon, who, like many Greek gods, had numerous wives.

Though neither Pegasus nor Bellerophon was ever to know
their true parental relationship, they came to love each other like brothers.
Thus, beyond the example of the bond that is possible between individual
and animal, the myth suggests that if humankind is to live in harmony with
nature, we must use love and respect, not force, to seek a better relationship
with one another.

Oil over watercolor was used for the full-color illustrations.
The text type is 18-point Koch Antiqua.

Published by Morrow Junior Books
a division of William Morrow and Company, Inc.
1350 Avenue of the Americas
New York, NY 10019
http://www.williammorrow.com

Printed in Hong Kong by South China Printing Company (1988) Ltd.

1 2 3 4 5 6 7 8 9 10

Library of Congress Cataloging-in-Publication Data
Mayer, Marianna.
Pegasus/as told by Marianna Mayer, illustrated by K. Y. Craft.
p. cm.
Summary: Retells how Bellerophon, son of the king of Corinth, secures the
help of the winged horse Pegasus in order to fight the monstrous Chimera.
ISBN 0-688-13382-7 (trade)—ISBN 0-688-13383-5 (library)
1. Pegasus (Greek mythology)—Juvenile literature.
[1. Pegasus (Greek mythology).
2. Mythology, Greek.]   I. Craft, Kinuko, ill.   II. Title.
BL820.P4M39 1998   398.2'0938'0454—DC20
96-32442   CIP AC

In memory of my beloved Max,
who possessed in life the spirit of Pegasus
and the heart of a hero....
Would that in death his soul might fly to Halcyon.
He will never be forgotten by those who love him.
1983-1996
M. M.

For Colin
The stars beckon brightly. Go and see!
K. Y. C.

here was a time long ago when the winged horse Pegasus roamed the heavenly land of Halcyon, as well as the earth below. No ordinary horse, Pegasus soared over mountains and galloped through clouds as effortlessly as he trotted across green meadows. Indeed, he was as free as the rushing wind that lifted his spreading wings.

The ancient gods of Greece loved him, calling Pegasus the poet's winged steed—the steed of inspiration. His hoof once struck the sweet grass of Halcyon, and from that spot water flowed, bestowing the power of creativity upon all who drank its waters. From that hour the three Muses—sisters of the Arts—tended that sacred spring and the ancient forest surrounding it.

A wild, solitary steed, Pegasus looked for no man's company—until the young hero Bellerophon went in search of him. This is their story.

NCE UPON A TIME, there was a heroic youth named Bellerophon, son of the king of Corinth, who had many enviable qualities. His bravery as a warrior was hailed throughout Greece. He was fair in his dealings and as handsome as any god.

Such fame brought him enemies as well as friends. One foe plotted against the innocent youth, succeeding in turning Bellerophon's good friend King Proetus against him. Foolishly believing that the young hero had fallen in love with his wife, Proetus planned revenge. He sent the unsuspecting Bellerophon to the king of Lycia with a sealed letter.

Now, the king of Lycia followed an ancient custom of hospitality—he never asked the reason for a guest's visit until ten days of feasting had passed. So when Bellerophon arrived, he was welcomed by the king and his family without question.

As the days went by, the youth and the king's youngest daughter, Philonoe, were never far apart. Love grew quickly, and Bellerophon was at the point of asking for the princess's hand in marriage when, on the tenth day, the king at last requested the reason the young man had come to Lycia. Only then did Bellerophon present his host with the letter.

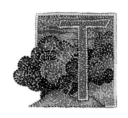he king took the letter and promptly broke the seal. Silently he read with horror these few simple words: PUT TO DEATH THE BEARER OF THIS MESSAGE.

Now, the king had grown very fond of Bellerophon. But he could not refuse King Proetus. If he did, he risked making the powerful Proetus his own enemy. Yet he was unwilling to bring about the youth's death by his own hand. Instead, he devised a dreadful task for the unsuspecting Bellerophon—a task the king knew would send him to certain death.

The next day, the king summoned Bellerophon and said, "I believe the gods have sent you to me, for my kingdom is in need of a hero."

"Ask what you will, Majesty. I am at your service," replied Bellerophon.

"Well said, noble youth. Your valor does you credit," answered the king. "The monster known as the Chimera terrorizes the people of Lycia. Already it has ravaged great portions of our land. The creature breathes fire from a lion's mouth and tears its victims with dragon claws. Every warrior who has gone to destroy it has perished. Will you be our champion and do battle with the monster?"

hough Bellerophon knew that he was being asked to go to his doom, he could hardly refuse the king without being considered a coward. But before setting out to challenge the monster, he asked the advice of a well-known soothsayer.

"You will fail like the others if you meet the beast upon the ground," declared the wise man. "Your only chance will be to convince the winged horse Pegasus to fly you to the Chimera's lair and there do battle in the air. For upon the back of this winged horse you might use your weapon to pierce the monster's heart. The Chimera can be killed no other way. But be warned: Pegasus is wild and unlikely to follow anyone."

Bellerophon journeyed to a place where the wise man had suggested he might catch a glimpse of the winged steed. "But expect no help from those who live nearby," the wise man had said. "The villagers guard their privacy and do not like strangers."

Many days and nights passed. As he wandered, Bellerophon asked time after time for news of Pegasus. But the answers were always the same: "Pegasus? There is no such animal!" The villagers laughed at him. "Go back from where it is you've come. You'll find no flying horse here."

Yet Bellerophon lingered, and finally he drifted off into the forest alone. There, as perhaps the gods intended, he stumbled upon the legendary fountain of Pirene.

U pon a stone slab beside the fountain Bellerophon read:

COME, WEARY TRAVELERS—DRINK AND BE REFRESHED—

FOR ONCE A WOMAN, PIRENE BY NAME, WEPT HERE

FOR HER ONLY CHILD, HER SON, WHO HAD BEEN SLAIN.

LONG DID PIRENE WEEP UNTIL SHE WAS TRANSFORMED

INTO AN ENDLESS STREAM OF FLOWING WATER.

PITYING THE POOR MOTHER, THE GODS HAVE SINCE BLESSED THIS

SPOT AND ALL THOSE WHO DRINK FROM THESE CRYSTAL WATERS.

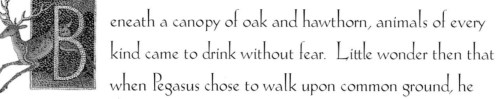eneath a canopy of oak and hawthorn, animals of every kind came to drink without fear. Little wonder then that when Pegasus chose to walk upon common ground, he favored this enchanted place. As Bellerophon approached, a pheasant flew from the marble rim of the fountain into a thicket. There was the sweet call of the goldfinch, and then silence. He leaned down, cupped his hand to catch the sweet water, and drank.

That night, with little idea of how to catch the elusive Pegasus, he decided to sleep nearby, out among the stars, the moon his only light.

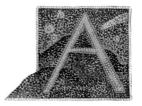s he slept, he dreamed that a luminous woman appeared holding a bridle so fine and pale that it was barely visible. "Noble youth, don't despair," said the woman. "Present Pegasus with this gift, and you'll not fail to win his love. If you learn its name, it will bind you both forever."

"Blessed goddess, I can barely see what you hold and do not know its name," said the youth.

"Its name is *trust*," replied the woman. "I give it to you to share with your brother, Pegasus. It will lie lightly between you, and none but the two of you will know it is there. Remember, you must be as equals if you are to succeed."

Now the bridle rested weightlessly in Bellerophon's hand. Then, as he gazed at it, the object melted into the air like a snowflake caught in his grasp. Looking up, Bellerophon hoped to question his benefactor further, but she too had disappeared.

The youth awoke to see that it was not yet dawn. The memory of his dream lingered while the distant village slept and a fog lay on the forest. He heard a sound. Bellerophon turned. There was a horse walking, all alone, upon the fallen leaves by the fountain, like a ghost that walks in moonlight.

The horse was watching him. Suddenly he felt akin to this lone animal who waited now, motionless, for his approach.

ellerophon drew near until they were a foot apart. Holding his breath, he tentatively reached out a hand.

The horse raised his forefeet off the ground and hurled himself upward. Suddenly a pair of magnificent wings spread from his broad shoulders. Now the steed was in the air, rising higher and higher, until he was far above the thunderstruck youth.

Pegasus circled the young man and then disappeared, obscured by a bank of clouds. But in a flash he reappeared, landing, wings folded, hardly winded, in front of Bellerophon. Pegasus pressed his velvet nose against the youth's shoulder, pushing him toward his flank, indicating that if the youth wished, he might ride.

The young man obeyed, and all at once they were climbing through the clouds. Holding tight to the horse's flowing mane, Bellerophon heard only the roar of the wind and the steady pounding of his own heart. They streaked across the sky, wildly dipping and weaving. Pegasus flew over jagged cliffs and followed a river that twisted and wound along like a shimmering silver snake.

The patient steed took time with the new rider. Though they were both till now solitary—Pegasus master of the clouds, the other a hero of the earth—together they learned the skill needed before challenging the Chimera.

t last one evening the youth gathered up his sword, spear, and shield and went to Pegasus. The stallion knew at once what was expected. He pounded the earth with his hooves. Snorting, he arched his neck and reared, eager for the young man to climb upon his back so that they might be off. Cloaked in darkness, the two flew up into the sky in search of the deadly monster.

The Chimera was the fiercest of beasts, with a goat's body joined to the head of a fire-breathing lion. Yet the monster had the iron-tough scales, tail, and claws of a dragon. Its lair was in a black cave on the side of a sheer cliff that plunged down to the sea. Descending only when hungry, the monster devoured people and animals at random and burned the countryside with its fiery breath.

It was nearly midnight when Pegasus brought the youth alongside the mouth of the cave. Suspended in midair, at first they waited, seeing only the charred bones of cattle and defeated warriors scattered about the entrance. A whisper of smoke curled upward from the opening and a choking stench filled the air, causing Pegasus to snort.

uddenly they heard a roar from inside the cave, and the Chimera sprang out. Fire burst from its mouth, and smoke engulfed both horse and rider. Turning, the Chimera whipped its dragon's tail at Pegasus. The winged stallion leapt nimbly to one side, allowing Bellerophon to swing his sword in a flashing arc, severing the tip of the monster's tail.

The Chimera gave a blood-chilling roar—never before had an opponent struck such a blow. Once more flames were flung at Bellerophon and Pegasus. Raising his shield, the hero deflected the flames, and a cascade of sparks shot in all directions, singeing Pegasus's mane and silver-tipped wings.

In the air, horse and rider were one motion, now swiftly rising, now swooping downward to escape each attack, anticipating each other's every move. The youth's sword struck out at the monster time after time, but the Chimera's powerful claws were too quick and the thick dragon scales a supreme defense against the warrior's attacks.

Bellerophon's arm grew numb as his heavy weapon clanged and railed in combat with the monster. Not for a moment could the youth let down his guard. He had to hold his shield high and keep his sword nimble if he was to ward off the monster. And then the Chimera broke through his defense—claws tore at the hero's arm. With lightning speed Pegasus soared out of harm's way, saving Bellerophon from certain death.

The battle raged on, and at daybreak, Bellerophon had not found a way to drive his sword into the monster's chest. Now he saw that he must make use of his spear if he was ever to succeed. Yet blinded by smoke and weakened from loss of blood, he continued to need both sword and shield to fend off the flames and deadly claws of the beast.

Bellerophon knew his strength was waning and time was running out for him. He must risk giving up his sword before all his power was spent. Letting down his defense but for a moment, he flung his sword away and took hold of his spear. Skillfully, he aimed and thrust with all his remaining might. Streaking through the air, the spear cut through smoke and fire and found its mark, piercing the monster to its very heart.

The monster's horrible roaring ceased, and the flames subsided. Now there was only silence as the lifeless body of the Chimera dropped from the rocky precipice. Falling thousands of feet to the raging sea below, it was swallowed by the waves and disappeared forever.

riumphant, horse and rider returned to the fountain of Pirene. And in this sacred spot, where a woman had once shed tears of loss, the hero turned to leave his beloved Pegasus. He knew he could not hold the stallion against his will. But as the earthbound Bellerophon watched Pegasus's alabaster wings catch the wind, lifting him toward the heavens, he hoped that this would not be the last he would see of his friend.

At the news that the Chimera had been slain there was great rejoicing. The king dared not attempt to harm the hero again, for he was now convinced that the gods favored Bellerophon. Instead, he gladly gave his consent to the marriage of his daughter and Bellerophon. The two were wed with much celebration and given a portion of the kingdom to rule together.

And though Bellerophon's duties were great and his marriage a source of happiness, as the years passed he found time enough to steal away from worldly things to seek his friend Pegasus whenever possible.

 s the goddess in his dream had foretold, the two had
become brothers, bonded by a trust that neither could
ever forget.